SMALLPOX

KEEP OUT OF THIS HOUSE

By Order of BOARD OF HEALTH

_____
HEALTH OFFICER

Any person removing this card without authority is liable to prosecution.

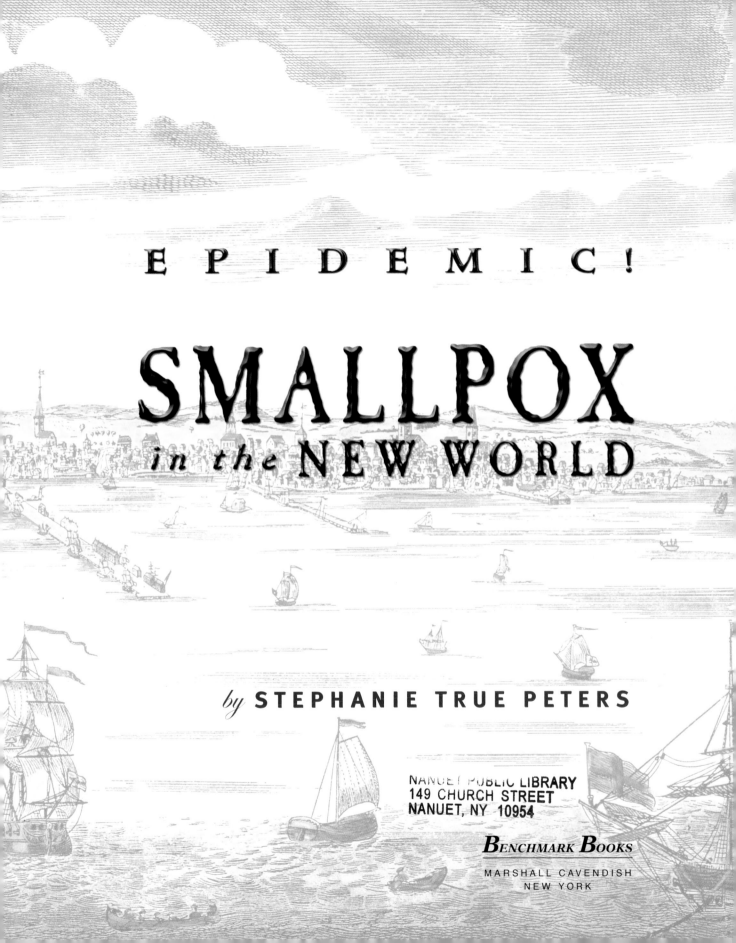

EPIDEMIC!

SMALLPOX
in the NEW WORLD

by STEPHANIE TRUE PETERS

BENCHMARK BOOKS

MARSHALL CAVENDISH
NEW YORK

ACKNOWLEDGMENTS

With thanks to Elizabeth A. Fenn, Assistant Professor of History,
Department of History, Duke University, for her careful reading of the manuscript.

Benchmark Books
Marshall Cavendish
99 White Plains Road
Tarrytown, New York 10591-9001
www.marshallcavendish.com

Book design by Michael Nelson

LIBRARY OF CONGRESS CATALOGING-IN-PUBLICATION DATA
Peters, Stephanie True, 1965-
Smallpox in the new world / by Stephanie True Peters.
p. cm. — (Epidemic!)
Summary: Describes the history of smallpox in the Americas,
covering the arrival of the Spanish as carriers, its spread throughout the New World,
the development of the smallpox vaccine, the elimination of the disease,
and its potential use as a terrorist weapon.
Includes bibliographical references and index.
ISBN 0-7614-1637-4
1. Smallpox—America—Juvenile literature.
[1. Smallpox. 2. Diseases.] I. Title. II. Series: Peters, Stephanie True, 1965- .
Epidemic!
RA644.S6P48 2004
616.9'12'0097—dc21
2003002646

Photo research by Linda Sykes Picture Research, Inc., Hilton Head, SC

Photo credits: front cover, 48: Jean-Loup Charmet/Science Photo Library/Photo Researchers, NY; i, 9 (top), 9 (bottom), 52, 60:
National Library of Medicine; ii, ix, 6, 7, 14, 16, 18, 19, 22, 27, 29, 30, 34, 40: The Granger Collection; vii: Archives
Charmet/Bridgeman Art Library, NY; x: National Library of Medicine/Photo Researchers, NY; 2: ©Gelderblom/Eye of
Science/Photo Researchers, NY; 3: Royal College of Surgeons, London, UK/Bridgeman Art Library, NY; 5, 47: Corbis; 12: National
Museum of History, Mexico City/Giraudon/Art Resource, NY; 21: Biblioteca Nacional, Madrid, Spain/Giraudon/Bridgeman Art
Library, NY; 25: New-York Historical Society/Bridgeman Art Library, NY; 26: Massachusetts Historical Society, Boston; 37:
Sheffield Galleries and Museums Trust, UK/Bridgeman Art Library, NY; 43: Scottish National Portrait Gallery; 44: Culver Pictures,
NY; 55: Smithsonian American Art Museum, Washington, DC/Art Resource, NY; Back cover: British Embassy, Mexico City,
Mexico/Bridgeman Art Library, NY

PRINTED IN CHINA

1 3 5 6 4 2

Front cover: 19th-century painting of a doctor vaccinating an infant
Back cover: 16th-century painting *The Taking of Tenochtitlán by Cortés*
Half title page: A warning sign posted on a San Francisco home in the early 1900s
Title page: Engraving of Boston Harbor around 1730
From the Author, page vii: 18th-century ceramic plaque *The Origin of Vaccination*

CONTENTS

FROM THE AUTHOR

The idea for a series of books about epidemics came to me while I was sitting in the doctor's office with my son. He had had a sleepless, feverish night. I suspected he had an ear infection and looked forward to the doctor confirming my diagnosis and prescribing antibiotics.

While waiting for the doctor to appear, I suddenly realized that the situation I was in—a mother looking to relieve her child's pain—was hardly new. Humans have had an ongoing battle against disease throughout history. Today we have tremendous knowledge of how the human body works. We understand how viruses and bacteria attack and how the body defends itself. Through immunizations and simple hygiene, we're often able to prevent disease in the first place. Our ancestors were not so knowledgeable, nor so lucky.

In this series, I have tried to put a human face on five epidemics that laid millions low. All five occurred in the past and have since been medically controlled. Yet in some areas of the world, similar stories are still being played out today as humans struggle against such enemies as AIDS, Ebola virus, hantavirus, and other highly contagious diseases. In the ongoing battle against disease, we may never have the upper hand. Microscopic foes are hard to fight.

The STORY of a KILLER

On May 8, 1980, the World Health Organization (WHO) made a stunning announcement. "Smallpox is dead!" proclaimed the headline of WHO's magazine. Smallpox, a deadly and disfiguring disease for which there is no known cure, had killed millions all over the world for centuries. Now it would kill no longer.

The campaign to eradicate smallpox began in 1967. WHO had attacked the disease in two ways. The first was mass vaccination. WHO's goal was to inject 80 percent of the world's population with the smallpox vaccine. Once vaccinated, these people would be immune to the disease for several years. Smallpox could not survive in a vaccinated community.

WHO's second method was known as surveillance-containment. Surveillance of at-risk communities helped detect an early outbreak of smallpox. Containment kept the disease from spreading. People with smallpox were quarantined, and anyone they had come into contact with was vaccinated.

Today the only known stores of smallpox virus are held

in two laboratories, one in Atlanta, Georgia, the other in Moscow, Russia. These labs are heavily protected with alarm systems and closed-circuit television. The vials of virus are frozen in liquid nitrogen. Removal of a vial requires two sets of keys that are held by different people.

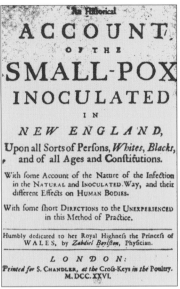

Dr. Zabdiel Boylston summed up his experience with smallpox and inoculation in this 1726 publication.

The smallpox virus is kept so that it can be studied. However, many argue that it should be destroyed. They fear that, despite the safeguards, the vials could fall into the wrong hands. Until the virus is truly eliminated, they say, there is always a chance that smallpox could accidentally escape or, worse, be used as a biological weapon. The terrorist attacks of September 11, 2001, have made many even more frightened of the possibility that this horrific disease could be purposely unleashed upon the world's population.

Although this is highly unlikely, history has shown us how catastrophic such an event would be. At its least destructive, smallpox killed 1 percent of the people it infected. At its worst, 90 percent of its victims may have died.

This book explores smallpox at its worst, when it wiped out hundreds of thousands of indigenous people in the Americas. It tells the story of how smallpox helped Europeans conquer and colonize the Americas—and, later, how the disease's devastating impact changed the map of the New World and nearly altered the course of the American Revolution. And finally, the book presents an overview of the history of smallpox itself, from its origins in the ancient world, to its control thanks to the tireless efforts of a few individuals, to its ultimate eradication from the face of the earth.

CHAPTER ONE

WHAT IS SMALLPOX?

Words indeed fail one when one tries to give a general picture of this disease.
—Thucydides, History of the Peloponnesian War

 MALLPOX IS CAUSED BY THE VARIOLA VIRUS, a member of the orthopox virus family. Orthopox viruses include cowpox and chicken pox. Humans can be infected by some of these pox viruses, but none are as deadly as smallpox.

When seen under an electron microscope, variola looks like a brick covered with points. It is one of the largest and most complicated viruses known, which may be what makes it so lethal and difficult to combat.

When variola invades a human cell, the cell is forced to reproduce the virus until there are hundreds of thousands of viruses inside it. When the cell can no longer contain the

Opposite:

Smallpox survivors were permanently scarred by the disease.

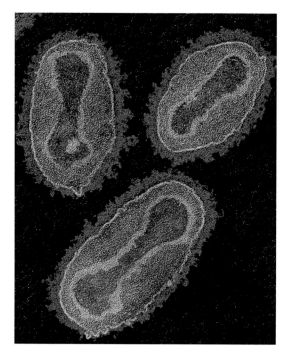

The variola virus, magnified 240,000 times by an electron microscope

viruses, the cell bursts. The viruses shower onto other cells, infecting them. Then the process starts all over again.

The variola virus has a twelve-day incubation period. During this time, an infected person shows no signs of illness. But within two weeks, it's clear that something isn't right.

The early symptoms of smallpox are headache, backache, high fever, and nausea. Four to five days later, a red rash appears on the face. As the disease worsens, the rash spreads down the body and turns into red blisters. The blisters fill with pus.

The pustules itch and burn so badly that the patient often feels as if he or she is on fire. Around the tenth day of the rash, the pustules burst, leaving the victim covered with oozing sores. These sores give off an odor like rotting flesh.

A few days later, the pustules dry into crusty yellow scabs that eventually fall off. The patient is left with deep-pitted scars, or pockmarks, where the scabs once were. Survivors are terribly disfigured, particularly their faces.

While the rash is spreading down the body, pus-filled sores form in the patient's mouth and throat. Swallowing is all but impossible. The virus sometimes attacks the eyes, leaving the victim partially or completely blind. Depending on the severity of the infection, the patient's heart, liver, and lungs can all be infected.

Death can occur at any time after the onset of the more severe symptoms. However, the patient is more likely to survive if the pustules are few and far between, a condition known as discrete smallpox. A patient's chances are much worse with confluent smallpox, when the sores are so close together that they touch. About 15 to 40 percent of patients with confluent smallpox die. The worst possible form of smallpox to get is hemorrhagic. In this case the patient bleeds from the nose and mouth and underneath the skin. Death is all but assured.

Smallpox is transmitted very quickly. A sneeze or a cough from an infected person sends thousands of virus-laden particles into the air. When other people inhale these particles, they become infected. Transmission can also occur if a person comes into contact with the pustules. Clothing, blankets, or other materials that have been on the body of a smallpox victim carry the disease. If other people use these items, they can become infected—and continue the chain of infection by sneezing or coughing or sharing clothes or blankets.

People who survive smallpox acquire immunity to the disease. When a virus such as variola strikes, the body generates antibodies to attack and kill it. If the patient survives the ill-

Pustules caused by cowpox, cousin to the more deadly smallpox

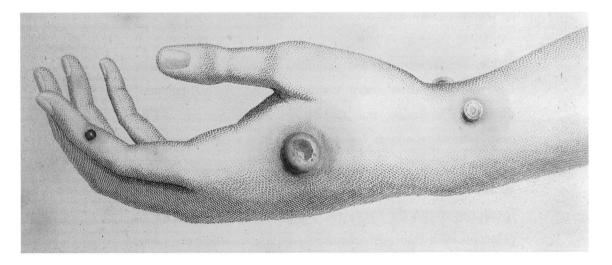

ness, the antibodies remain in the body, ready to attack. Acquiring immunity is the only sure protection against variola; even today, with all the advancements of modern medicine, there is no known cure for smallpox. Vaccination is the only preventative.

THE ORIGIN OF SMALLPOX

The variola virus can be traced back to prehistoric times. In its early form it was a virus that infected rodents. Prehistoric humans hunted rodents for food or came into contact with them in other ways. At some point, the virus jumped from rodents to humans.

The virus might have died out or mutated to coexist with humans if prehistoric humans had remained hunter-gatherers. Hunter-gatherers lived in very small groups that had little contact with one another. So while one group could be wiped out by the virus, others would be able to remain safe. However, around 9000 B.C. humans began to cultivate crops and settle into larger communities. Now when the virus struck, it could move from person to person without exhausting its supply of hosts. Since the virus could survive without coexisting with its host, it had no need to mutate into a kinder, gentler virus.

As humankind evolved and developed over the centuries, so did the smallpox virus, until it was completely different from the virus that had jumped from the rodents. Now it was specifically designed to invade and infect human cells.

EARLY HISTORY

Most researchers agree that smallpox originated in central Africa sometime around 10,000 B.C. By 8000 B.C., it had settled in the Fertile Crescent, the region in the Middle East surrounding the Tigris and Euphrates Rivers where the earliest civilizations developed. From then on, smallpox appeared wherever human populations dwelled in large numbers.

Ancient Egyptian documents dating back as early as 3000 B.C. mention a disease that sounds much like smallpox. Records written around 1500 B.C. indicate that smallpox had reached India by that time, probably first arriving in that region with Egyptian traders.

Egyptians may also have passed the disease on to the Hittite empire. The Hittites were an Indo-European people who flourished in Asia Minor from 1600 B.C. to 1200 B.C. Ancient documents state that around 1350 B.C., while at war with Egypt, the Hittites were struck by a deadly epidemic that nearly destroyed their empire. Many scholars believe the disease was smallpox, passed to Hittite soldiers from Egyptian prisoners.

Such documents provide written evidence that smallpox existed in the ancient world. In addition, there may be one stunning piece of physical evidence. The mummified remains of Egyptian pharaoh Ramses V, who died in 1157 B.C., show pockmarks on his face and hands. Most scholars agree that these look like smallpox scars.

From Egypt and the surrounding regions, the disease may

Ancient cultures performed elaborate rituals to ward off smallpox. This is a picture of an Indian ceremony.

have made its way to Greece. Thucydides, a Greek historian (460–401 B.C.), described symptoms of a smallpox-like disease that struck Athens in 430 B.C.:

"People in perfect health suddenly began to have burning feelings in the head. . . . Their eyes became red and inflamed; inside their mouths there was bleeding from the throat and tongue, and the breath became unnatural and unpleasant. . . . The skin was rather reddish and livid, breaking out into small pustules and ulcers. . . . The disease, first settling in the head, went on to affect every part of the body in turn, and even when people escaped its worst effects, it still left its traces on them."

Athens had been winning a war against a neighboring city-state, Sparta, when the disease struck. The Spartans defeated their weakened rival soon after. Athens never regained its power.

In A.D. 164 the Roman army picked up a disease while on a campaign in southwestern Asia. The sickness spread quickly through the ranks until the Romans were forced to retreat. They brought the malady home with them when they returned. For fifteen years the disease, called the Plague of Antonine after emperor Marcus Aurelius Antoninus (121–180), swept through the empire. Historians estimate that the death toll ranged from 3½ million to 7 million people. Marcus Aurelius may have been one of the epidemic's victims.

Marcus Aurelius's physician, a Greek named Galen (129–199), left a brief description of the Plague of Antonine that included high fever, pus-filled sores that dried into scabs, pockmarking after the scabs fell off, and sores in the

Galen's writings, including his observations of diseases, influenced the practice of medicine for centuries.

Galien natif de Pergame ville d'Asie, excellent Medecin viuoit du temps des Empereurs Antonin le Philosophe et de Commodus, on tient qu'il a vescu 140 ans.

SMALLPOX *in the* NEW WORLD

mouth and throat. He believed that he was seeing the same disease that Thucydides had described. But was either or both of these diseases smallpox? Historians aren't positive because the symptoms described match other diseases, such as measles.

Around A.D. 250 the Chinese were laid low by a disease they called the Hunpox. The disease was named after the Huns, a nomadic people from central Asia, who brought it with them when they invaded China. The Huns probably contracted the disease in their travels across the continent. Again, we don't know for sure if Hunpox was smallpox because the existing descriptions of the disease are vague.

Historians are more convinced that the epidemic that struck northern China around the year 310 was smallpox. Ko Hung (281–340), a Chinese alchemist-pathologist, left a clear description of the disease:

"Recently there have been persons suffering from epidemic sores which attack the head, face and trunk. In a short time these sores spread all over the body. They have the appearance of hot boils containing some white matter. While some of these pustules are drying up a fresh crop appears. If not treated early the patients usually die. Those who recover are disfigured with purplish scars which do not fade until after a year."

Smallpox made its next devastating appearance in A.D. 570

A young Chinese girl shows the ravages of smallpox.

during a conflict known as the Elephant War. According to the Koran, the sacred text of Islam, the disease struck down huge numbers of troops from Abyssinia (modern-day Ethiopia) as they were marching to Mecca to face their Arab enemies. The Abyssinian troops were so weakened that the Arabs were able to rout them—and their elephants—from their city.

Ten years later, Greek soldiers who had recently been in the Middle East brought a highly infectious disease to southern France and northern Italy. Gregory, bishop of Tours, left this description of that epidemic:

"A person, after being seized with a violent fever, was covered all over with vesicles and small pustules. . . . The vesicles were white, hard, unyielding, and very painful. If the patient survived to their maturation, they broke, and began to discharge, when the pain was greatly increased by the adhesion of the clothes to the body."

In 583 China passed a smallpox-like disease on to Korea via trade routes. Two years later, Buddhist monks from Korea carried the infection into Japan.

Were all these epidemics smallpox or some other disease with similar symptoms? Historians aren't sure because so many records from this time called deadly diseases "the plague," regardless of their symptoms. Around 910, however, a Persian physician named Rhazes (864–c. 925) wrote a treatise distinguishing smallpox from measles. (Measles caused fever and a red blistering rash much like smallpox.) Rhazes's treatise became the definitive description of smallpox. Chroniclers would no longer confuse the disease with any other. Anyone reading a history of an epidemic would now know for certain if it was smallpox or not.

Opposite:

Top: Sitala, the Indian goddess of smallpox
Bottom: The demon Smallpox flees the brave Japanese warrior Yoritomo.

WORSHIPING SMALLPOX

Many diverse religions have gods, goddesses, and saints of smallpox. Some of these gods and goddesses have been around since ancient times; others appeared later in history. Their existence helps prove the presence of smallpox throughout the world.

The Hindu goddess of smallpox, Sitala, appeared in India sometime before the first millennium B.C. Her name means "the cool one." When Sitala entered your body, you had to appease her by eating and drinking only cooling foods and liquids. When she left, you were either dead or stronger for having survived her possession.

T'ou-Shen Niang Niang, the Chinese goddess of smallpox, appeared in the eleventh century. This goddess was supposed to enjoy giving smallpox to young children with beautiful faces. If the children survived, their faces would be forever disfigured, a sign of the goddess's power. Parents used to cover their children's faces with ugly paper masks at night in the hope that T'ou-Shen Niang Niang would pass the children by.

In Japan the smallpox goddess was called Hoso-No-Kami. In West Africa the Dahomey people worshiped a god called Sakpata, while the neighboring Yoruba called their smallpox god Obaluaiye. Worshipers in Sri Lanka (formerly Ceylon) visited the temple of Pattini in the hopes of avoiding the disease.

Saint Nicaise is the patron saint of smallpox in the Catholic religion. Nicaise was a bishop in Reims, France. He stood up to and was beheaded by German invaders around A.D. 451. He supposedly carried his head to his church steps before dying. He became the patron saint of smallpox because he had survived the disease just the previous year. People living in the Middle Ages would call upon him in their prayers as a way of warding off the disease:

"In the name of our Lord Jesus Christ, may the Lord protect these persons, and . . . ward off the smallpox. St. Nicaise had the smallpox, and he asked the Lord [to preserve] whoever carried his name inscribed: O St. Nicaise! Thou illustrious bishop and martyr, pray for me a sinner, and defend me by thy intercession from this disease. Amen."

Smallpox continued to spread and destroy. Denmark and Iceland were infected in the mid-1200s. A colony on Greenland was wiped out in 1430. An estimated 50,000 people died in a 1438 epidemic in Paris. Nagasaki, Japan, lost more than 2,000 people in 1613.

Despite these outbreaks, most scholars agree that by the 1500s smallpox was endemic to Europe, Asia, and parts of Africa. When a disease is endemic, it is always present in a society. It has enough new hosts to remain alive, but enough people have immunity that the society survives as well. If a disease is endemic long enough, future generations can develop a resistance to it. Their reaction to the disease that killed their great-great-grandparents is much less severe.

An epidemic, on the other hand, moves in, wipes out a vast number, then dies out. The worst epidemics occur in societies that have never had contact with the disease before.

At the end of the fifteenth century, Europeans introduced variola into just such societies. As we shall see, the results were devastating.

CHAPTER TWO

SMALLPOX CONQUERS MEXICO *and* SOUTH AMERICA

*It became so great a pestilence among them throughout the land that in most
provinces more than half the population died; in others the proportion
was little less. . . . They died in heaps, like bedbugs.*
—Toribio Motolinia, a Spanish monk who witnessed
the smallpox epidemic that struck the Aztecs

IN 1492 CHRISTOPHER COLUMBUS convinced King Ferdinand and Queen Isabella of Spain that he could find a west-to-east sea route to the Far East. Like most European countries, Spain wanted ready access to the wealth—the spices, silk, and exotic materials—found in the East. With this goal in mind, the king and queen agreed to fund Columbus's voyage across the Atlantic.

Columbus's four subsequent voyages and the "discovery" of the Americas opened the door for future Europeans. They didn't travel empty-handed. They brought things that amazed and terrified the native populations, such as horses and guns. But it was the unseen passenger, smallpox, that eventually caused the greatest horror.

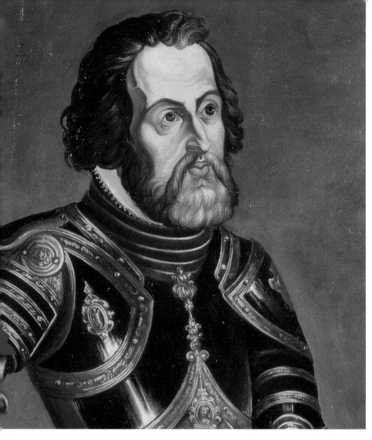

Portrait of Hernán
Cortés, Spanish
conquistador

SMALLPOX SWEEPS THE ISLANDS

When Columbus landed on the island of Hispaniola (now the Dominican Republic and Haiti) in December of 1492, the indigenous people, the Arawak, numbered about one million. Over the course of the next sixty years, the population would be reduced to fewer than five hundred people. What happened during those years to cause such widespread devastation?

Soon after Columbus left Hispaniola, Spanish conquistadores came to the island to seize the gold that had been discovered there. Over the next two decades, the Spanish forced the native population to mine the precious metal for them. Hard labor, dangerous mining conditions, and brutal treatment by the Spanish killed many.

Starvation was another cause of death. Because they were working the mines, the Arawak could no longer tend to their fields. As a result, the crops failed. Several seasons of poor harvests led to a scarcity of food. Those who survived starvation were malnourished, weak, and vulnerable to infection. The Spanish had brought many new diseases with them, but none proved to be as devastating to the Arawak as smallpox.

Variola disembarked with newly arriving colonists from Spain in 1507. The Arawak had never been exposed to variola before. They fell dead by the hundreds as the epidemic swept the island.

A second epidemic struck Hispaniola in 1518. This time it came not from Spain but from Africa.

By 1518 most of the gold had been mined from the

island. Now the Spanish were growing sugarcane, a very labor-intensive crop. The population of Hispaniola was so depleted that the Spanish brought African slaves to the island. Some of the slaves had smallpox.

The Arawak had no more resistance to smallpox in 1518 than they had had in 1507. Again the disease struck with great ferocity, killing much of the remaining population. The Arawak would never recover.

As the Spanish continued their exploration—and exploitation—of the islands neighboring Hispaniola, smallpox traveled along with them. Thousands of native Cubans died when smallpox struck their island in 1518. From Cuba the disease jumped to Puerto Rico. It took just a few months in 1519 for it to kill more than half of that island's population.

Such massive deaths made it easy for Spain to assume control of the islands. A man named Diego Velázquez was appointed governor of Cuba. Velázquez's secretary was Hernán Cortés. It was Cortés who inadvertently helped spread smallpox to the greatest nation yet seen in the New World: the Aztecs.

CORTÉS AND THE AZTECS

In 1519 the Aztec empire stretched more than 200,000 square miles, covering an area that included much of modern central Mexico, Guatemala, and El Salvador. Five to six million people lived within its boundaries. A single, all-powerful emperor ruled the nation.

The Aztec capital city, Tenochtitlán (today's Mexico City), had been built in 1325 on an island surrounded by a large lake. It was connected to the mainland by broad causeways. At its center was a grand temple for worshiping the many Aztec

Tenochtitlán, the Aztec capital city, before its fall to the Spanish

gods. Religious practices, including human sacrifice, were at the heart of the Aztec culture.

Governor Velázquez had heard rumors of the vast wealth of the Aztecs. In late 1518 he decided to send Cortés to Mexico to explore the area and report back his findings. But as Cortés prepared for his journey, Velázquez became suspicious that Cortés planned to conquer the Aztecs and keep the wealth of that empire for himself. Velázquez ordered Cortés to stay in Cuba.

But by now Cortés was hungry for the riches said to exist in Mexico. He disobeyed Velázquez's order and on February 18, 1519, set sail with five hundred and fifty soldiers, one hundred sailors, sixteen horses, and a dozen or so guns and cannon.

After a few brief stops, Cortés and his men landed near the settlement of Potonchán. They were met by native people bearing small gifts of gold. The natives advised the Spanish to take the gifts and leave. Cortés refused, and the meeting turned into a bloody conflict that left Cortés in control of the area.

From there Cortés began his slow but steady advance on his ultimate goal: the capture of the Aztec capital, Tenochtitlán. Tenochtitlán lay two hundred miles inland. To reach it, Cortés and his men would have to make their way through dangerous and unfamiliar terrain. They would also face potentially deadly confrontations with the region's inhabitants.

Not all of Cortés's men wanted to pursue this course. They insisted that they turn back and return to Cuba. Cortés, knowing he would be imprisoned in Cuba for having defied

Velázquez, deliberately sank his own ships. With their only means of returning to Cuba cut off, the disgruntled Spaniards had no choice but to continue with Cortés.

The Spanish soon came into contact with a longtime enemy of the Aztecs, the Tlaxcalans. After defeating the Tlaxcalans, Cortés convinced them to fight with the Spanish against the Aztecs. Together, the Spanish and Tlaxcalans pressed on toward Tenochtitlán.

The chances of capturing Tenochtitlán seemed slim. The Aztecs had an army of thousands. Even with the addition of the Tlaxcalans, the Spanish were far outnumbered. However, the power of Spanish guns and horses more than made up for their small force.

Few of the natives had ever seen or heard of such weapons and animals before. They fell to the ground in terror when Cortés gave a demonstration of what they could do. One of the men who witnessed this demonstration was a messenger from Tenochtitlán. He reported what he had seen to Montezuma II, the Aztec emperor.

Montezuma had been fearful of the Spanish even before the messenger made his report. Part of his fear came from his belief that he was destined to lose his empire that very year. Omens, dreams of ruin, and the anticipated return of Quetzalcoatl, a pale, bearded Aztec god who despised human sacrifice, had haunted him for months. When Montezuma heard a description of Cortés—a man with white skin and a black beard—he believed it was Quetzalcoatl.

Thus, when Cortés's band finally reached the outskirts of Tenochtitlán on November 8, 1519, Montezuma greeted them with gifts of gold and jewels, welcoming them into his city. He would soon regret his openness, however, for within

Montezuma's representatives welcomed Cortés with gifts; Cortés repaid this trust by ousting the Aztec ruler shortly thereafter.

two weeks Cortés had placed him under arrest and assumed control of the capital.

In the months that followed, the Aztecs in and around Tenochtitlán became increasingly resentful of the Spanish. The Spanish made constant demands for gold and other wealth. In addition, they horrified the Aztecs by destroying sacred statues of Aztec gods and defiling their temples. Although the Spanish managed to keep control of the capital, tensions between the Aztecs and the invaders grew.

Then, in April 1520, Cortés received news that a Spanish expedition had landed in Mexico. The expedition, led by Pánfilo de Narváez, had been sent by Governor Velázquez to arrest Cortés.

Cortés immediately departed Tenochtitlán to meet the force. He left a man named Alvarado in charge of the capital. Cortés succeeded in defeating Narváez, but upon his return to Tenochtitlán in June, he discovered that Alvarado had lost control of the city after disrupting a sacred Aztec ceremony. Outraged Aztecs had risen up against the Spanish and now held them captive.

Cortés tried to regain the upper hand. He entered the city reinforced with troops from Narváez's expedition and forced

Montezuma to speak on behalf of the Spanish. But the Aztecs no longer respected the emperor's position and threw stones and arrows at him. He died as a result of his injuries.

Hostilities escalated between the Spanish and the Aztecs. Finally, the Aztecs managed to rout the Spanish from their city once and for all. Realizing they were overpowered, the Spanish fled—but not before more than six hundred of them had been killed in a bloody battle known as *noche triste*, the night of tears. Dead bodies of Spanish soldiers lay strewn about the streets of the city. One of those bodies held a deadly secret.

When Narváez's expedition set sail from Cuba, it had on board an enslaved African named Francisco de Baguía. De Baguía had smallpox. He passed the disease on to a Spanish soldier. This soldier was one of the casualties left behind when the Spanish fled Tenochtitlán. The Aztecs caught smallpox when handling his corpse.

A Spanish monk, Fray Toribio Motolinia, witnessed the epidemic that swept through the Aztec population in the fall of 1520 and winter of 1521:

"The victims were so covered with pustules . . . it extended over all parts of their bodies. Over the forehead, head, chest. It was very destructive. . . . Many of the survivors were pockmarked . . . some were blind. . . . This pestilence lasted sixty days, sixty lamentable days."

Smallpox appears to have killed half the Aztec population in less than six months, leaving a once mighty empire much weakened. It also rocked the Aztecs' beliefs in their gods. When Cortés and his men had first arrived, they were horrified to discover that the Aztecs practiced human sacrifice. The Spaniards warned that their God would punish the Aztecs for this practice. The Aztecs at first were outraged.

The Aztecs left a record in pictures of the epidemic. In the center of this drawing lie the dead, blanketed in shrouds. At right, two men, covered in pustules, struggle with the disease.

Then smallpox struck—but it killed mainly Aztecs and only a few Spanish. Why would this be? The Aztecs came to believe that the Spanish God was stronger than their gods. They began to question the very heart of their religion.

Despite the ravages of smallpox, the Aztecs still might have defeated the Spanish if they had had a strong leader. But Montezuma was dead—killed by his own people—before the epidemic fully hit. His successor, Cuitláhuac, was a fierce warrior determined to rid his land of the invaders. Unfortunately for the Aztecs, he was one of the first to fall from smallpox. The twenty-five-year-old nephew who succeeded him simply couldn't win against smallpox and the Spanish.

Meanwhile, the deadly disease was raging through smaller Mexican tribes outside of the Aztec empire. Whenever Cortés found a leaderless tribe, he assumed control. Thus he gathered more allies in his fight against the Aztecs.

In August 1521, after a three-month siege, Tenochtitlán fell to the Spanish. Cortés had beaten the Aztecs from without. Smallpox had beaten them from within. Demoralized, depopulated, and utterly defeated, the Aztec empire collapsed. Mexico and all its riches were now in the hands of the Spanish.

FRANCISCO PIZARRO AND THE INCAS

In 1522 rumors of a vast empire along the west coast of South America reached Francisco Pizarro. Pizarro was a Spanish conquistador who had explored and settled in Panama in 1519. Now he would turn his sights on the Inca empire.

It would take him more than a decade to achieve his goal of conquering the Incas. Expeditions in 1524 and 1526 failed because Pizarro's small forces were too weak to combat the huge Inca army. He launched his third and final expedition in 1531, supported with fresh funds from the Spanish monarchy.

The Inca empire covered what is now Peru, Ecuador, Bolivia, northern Chile, and part of Argentina. Historians estimate that as many as sixteen million people lived in this vast region. The center of the king-dom, Cuzco, was located in the Andes Mountains. A sophis-ticated system of roads linked Cuzco to the rest of the empire and allowed the emperor and his soldiers to travel freely within its boundaries.

Roads lead travelers from Cuzco, the center of the Inca empire.

The roads also carried information. Messengers probably brought news of the Aztecs' defeat along these roads. In 1524 the roads carried a different kind of messenger: the messenger of death. Smallpox had made its way from Mexico through Central America to South America, where it traveled along the roads until it touched every corner of the Inca empire. The dis-ease raged for three years, reaching Cuzco in 1527.

The ruler of the Incas during this epidemic was Huayna Capac. When Cuzco was struck, Huayna Capac was in Quito (today the capital of Ecuador), one thousand miles north. He left for Cuzco at once. Along the way, messengers from Cuzco reported the deaths of Huayna Capac's brother, sister, uncle, and a powerful general. Before his journey was through, Huayna Capac had caught the disease.

Huayna Capac secluded himself once he reached Cuzco. "My father the Sun is calling me," he told his people. "I shall go now to rest at his side." He died alone, leaving the fate of the empire in the hands of his successor, his son Ninan Cuyoche.

But Ninan Cuyoche would not live to rule. He died of smallpox soon after his father.

Next in line for the throne was Huayna Capac's other son, Huáscar. Huáscar was the legitimate son of Huayna Capac and his queen. However, Huayna Capac had another son, Atahualpa. Atahualpa's mother was not the queen, which made his claim to the throne illegitimate. Still, he had been a favorite of Huayna Capac. When Huayna Capac died, Atahualpa challenged Huáscar for the throne.

By killing first the emperor and then his chosen heir, smallpox had brought the Incas into a civil war that raged for five years. Atahualpa emerged victorious from the conflict, but the empire was never the same. The number of people who died in the war is unknown. More than 200,000 are believed to have succumbed to smallpox. Hand in hand, disease and civil war divided, killed, and demoralized the population.

This was the stage onto which Pizarro strode in 1532. With only six hundred men, he defeated Atahualpa's forces, then captured and executed Atahualpa. Without a leader, Cuzco fell easily. Pizarro took control of the city in 1533.

That same year, smallpox struck Quito. It struck again in 1535. By that time, the Inca empire was firmly in the hands of the Spanish. The Incas, like the Aztecs, never regained control.

It took less than two decades for the Aztecs, then the Incas, to fall. Smallpox alone did not defeat them. The Spanish had superior weapons and a boldness brought on by the promise of immense wealth. However, there can be

This genealogy of Inca rulers shows the abrupt change to Spanish rule after Pizarro's conquest.

no doubt that smallpox made it easier for a mere 1,200 men to conquer several million.

The conquered empires were never the same. Christianity replaced the native religions. Spaniards married natives and produced families of mixed heritage. The indigenous people became akin to slaves, working in the mines and fields to provide wealth for their Spanish conquerors. What remained of their own economies collapsed as a result.

Smallpox continued to haunt Central and South America. Epidemics struck Peru in 1558 and again in 1585. A witness to the 1585 outbreak left these words describing what he saw:

"They died by scores and hundreds. Villages were depopulated. Corpses were scattered over the fields or piled up in the houses or huts. All branches of industrial activity were paralyzed. The fields were uncultivated; the herds were untended. . . . [Many] escaped the foul disease, but only to be wasted by famine."

Soon, unsuspecting native people in other parts of the New World would witness such grim scenes. Smallpox had probably been working its way farther into North America during the same decades it was decimating the Aztec and Inca populations. By the early seventeenth century, it would make its presence felt.

CHAPTER THREE

SMALLPOX *and the* EARLY AMERICAN COLONIES

A few straggling inhabitants, burial places, empty wigwams, and some skeletons.
—*Scene found at Plymouth by Miles Standish in 1620*

PAIN AND, TO A LESSER EXTENT, PORTUGAL had control over Mexico and Central and South America by the late 1500s. Florida came under Spanish rule in 1565, when Spain seized the French settlement of Fort Caroline and renamed the post Saint Augustine. Saint Augustine became the first permanent European colony in North America. By 1610 Spain had also established the colony of Santa Fe, New Mexico, in the southwestern region of what is now the United States.

Europeans from other countries began coming to the New World soon afterward. In 1607 England founded its first successful colony at Jamestown, Virginia. French explorer Samuel

Opposite:

Countless Indians, like this Mandan woman, died during the smallpox epidemics that swept the New World.

de Champlain set up the first trading post in Canada at the future site of Quebec City in 1608. In 1609 Henry Hudson sailed up the river that would bear his name, giving the Dutch claim over what would later become New York. Spain continued to focus its efforts in the west and southwest, establishing settlements in modern-day California, Arizona, and Texas.

Many early expeditions to the New World were made in search of wealth and to set up trading posts. Later, settlers would come to colonize, hoping for lives with more freedom and possibility. But what of the people who already lived in the New World?

At the start of the seventeenth century, more than 20 million Native Americans were living in North America. By 1679 that number would be greatly reduced. Skirmishes between enemy tribes and with Europeans over land caused some deaths. Smallpox and other diseases caused a great many more.

Smallpox wormed its way northward from Mexico with the Spanish and also traveled across the Atlantic with the French, English, and Dutch. In the East, it spread along the New England coastlands, then journeyed up waterways as the Europeans ventured inland. There and in the West, it attacked Native Americans both physically and mentally, for with each new outbreak, the memories of the few who survived were stamped with horrific images of their loved ones dying in agony.

SMALLPOX STRIKES THE NATIVE POPULATION

In 1617 the first epidemic swept through the native tribes living along the Massachusetts coast. When it ended in 1619, nine-tenths of those who caught smallpox had died from the infection.

The Indians had never seen a disease like smallpox before. It's impossible to imagine the anguish and terror they must have felt as the silent killer struck again and again. There would have been scarcely enough people left standing to tend the crops or care for the sick. Entire tribes and their cultures—the Massachuset, the Abenaki, the Pawtucket, the Wampanoag—were virtually wiped out because of smallpox and starvation.

The Pilgrims landed in Plymouth one year after the epidemic ended. They survived their first year in Massachusetts because of the generosity and aid of Wampanoags. But relations between the colonists and the Native Americans didn't remain peaceful. Throughout the next decade, conflicts over the use of land and the Pilgrims' desire to convert the Indians to Christianity created an increasingly tense situation.

In 1630 new shiploads of English arrived in Massachusetts. Like the Pilgrims, these passengers came to the New World seeking religious freedom. Known as Puritans, they were the first of many groups to cross the Atlantic in what was later called the Great Migration.

God-fearing Pilgrims brought Christianity —and smallpox—to native populations.

Increase Mather believed God was eradicating Indians with smallpox so that Europeans could settle the land.

The relationship between the Native Americans and the English settlers was still uneasy in 1630. Then, in 1633, a second smallpox epidemic struck Massachusetts. Many of the Native Americans who had survived the earlier epidemic died. Twenty Plymouth colonists also succumbed.

Despite these twenty deaths, the 1633 epidemic was seen as a gift from God by some Puritans. One such Puritan was Increase Mather, an outspoken clergyman and one of the first presidents of Harvard College. He wrote this of the outbreak:

"The Indians began to be quarrelsome concerning the bounds of the land they had sold to the English; but God ended the controversy by sending the smallpox amongst the Indians at Saugust, who were before that time exceeding numerous. Whole towns of them were swept away, in some of them not so much as one Soul escaping the destruction."

Mather was not alone in his belief that smallpox was a beneficent act of God. Records remain of many European settlers praising God for the disease. By wiping out the Indians, smallpox helped the colonists help themselves to land and resources formerly controlled by unfriendly native people. The Europeans could and did colonize virtually unchallenged in some areas.

Smallpox did not stay confined to the shores of Massachusetts. At the time of the 1633 epidemic, Dutch traders were on the Massachusetts coast looking to establish trade relations with the Native American tribes. The Dutch retreated inland when the epidemic struck.

They carried smallpox along with them. Their journey took them through the Connecticut River valley. In the winter of 1633–1634, the disease attacked the Narraganset Indians as well as other tribes living along the Connecticut River.

William Bradford, governor of the Plymouth colony, happened to be in the area when the epidemic hit. He described what he saw during this outbreak:

"They lye on their hard matts, ye poxe breaking and mattering, and running one into another, their skin cleaving (by reason thereof) to the matts they lye on; when they turn them, a whole side will flea off at once . . . and they will be all of a gore blood, most fearful to behold. And then being very sore, what with could [cold] and other distempers, they dye like rotten sheep." The death toll was horrific: "Of a 1000, above 900 and a halfe of them dyed," Bradford later wrote, "and many of them did rott above ground for want of buriall."

It didn't take long for the disease to spread throughout and beyond the boundaries of New England. By 1640 it had reached upstate New York and central Ontario. Many Europeans sickened and died, but the Native Americans who lived in these areas suffered the most.

The Iroquois League of upstate New York was a coalition of five tribes: the Cayuga, the Oneida, the Onondaga, the Seneca, and the Mohawk. Its population numbered around 20,000 people in 1640. The Iroquois' longtime enemy, the Huron Confederacy of central Ontario, was an alliance of four tribes and had between 30,000 and 40,000 people. Then smallpox struck.

Smallpox wiped out entire villages of Native Americans, leaving only a few survivors to mourn and bury the dead.

The Hurons recognized that the malady was something new, brought to them through contact with people from outside their tribes:

"This disease has not been engendered here; it comes from without; never have we seen demons so cruel. The other maladies lasted two or three moons; this has been persecuting us more than a year. [Our diseases] are content [to kill] one or two in a family; this, in many, has left no more than that number and in many none at all."

Smallpox ravaged the Huron Confederacy for seven years. By 1647 the Hurons' numbers had dwindled to fewer than ten thousand. The disease had likewise weakened the Iroquois—though not as much as it had their Huron rivals.

In 1648 the Iroquois League launched and won a decisive campaign against the Hurons. The once powerful Huron Confederacy fell apart, and its members scattered to other regions. Three hundred fled north to Quebec. A thousand more merged with tribes living along the Great Lakes. An unknown number of others were absorbed into the Iroquois nations.

The Iroquois were ravaged by smallpox again in 1649, 1663, and 1679. Unlike the Huron, the Iroquois managed to hold their confederation together. Still, the effects of repeated attacks from such a horrifying disease were felt throughout their territory. As the governor of Canada described:

"The small pox desolates them to such a degree, that they think no longer of meeting nor of wars, but only of bewailing the dead, of whom there is already an immense number."

THE VULNERABLE COLONISTS

While Native Americans were dying by the thousands, shiploads of new settlers were arriving regularly from Europe,

An Exact Prospect of CHARLESTOWN, the Metropolis of the Province of SOUTH CAROLINA.

increasing the white population. Settlements developed into complex towns. Boston, New York, Philadelphia, Jamestown, and Charleston grew into bustling centers of trade. Second and third generations of children were born who had never set foot in Europe.

Many European settlers arrived in the New World as indentured servants, people who had agreed to work for a number of years in exchange for passage across the Atlantic. Laborers from another part of the world were also coming to America by the mid-1600s—but not by choice. The slave trade between Africa and America had become brisk; new shipments of Africans were arriving regularly. Smallpox arrived with Africans and Europeans alike.

Smallpox had been endemic, or always present, in Europe and Africa for generations. Because the populations in these societies were large and lived in close quarters, the virus had enough new hosts—usually young children and infants—to infect so that it survived. But at the same time, enough people had acquired immunity to variola that the society survived smallpox as well.

Port cities such as Charleston (formerly Charlestown) were hotbeds of commerce—and infectious diseases such as smallpox.

TO BE SOLD on board the Ship *Bance-Ysland*, on tuesday the 6th of *May* next, at *Ashley-Ferry*; a choice cargo of about 250 fine healthy

NEGROES,

just arrived from the Windward & Rice Coast. —The utmost care has already been taken, and shall be continued, to keep them free from the least danger of being infected with the SMALL-POX, no boat having been on board, and all other communication with people from *Charles-Town* prevented.

Austin, Laurens, & Appleby.

N. B. Full one Half of the above Negroes have had the SMALL-POX in their own Country.

Slave ships were known to carry smallpox with their human cargo.

Not so the second and third generations of colonists. The communities in America were still too small for smallpox to become endemic. Outbreaks would occur periodically, but there were too few hosts to keep the virus alive. Years would pass without an epidemic. Like the Native Americans, many colonists grew up never having been exposed to the virus. They were sitting ducks whenever smallpox sailed into port with the Europeans and Africans. And this it did with appalling regularity.

Boston in particular suffered. Six major epidemics hit the town in the seventeenth century: in 1636, 1659, 1666, 1677–1678, 1689–1690, and 1697–1698. The 1677–1678 epidemic killed as many as thirty people in one day alone. The minister of Boston's Old South Church, Thomas Thacher, was so shocked by the devastation that he published a broadside he hoped would help people tackle the disease. This broadside, entitled *A Brief rule to guide the Common-People of New-England How to order themselves and theirs in the Small Pocks, or Measles,* was the first medical publication in America.

Most people by this time knew that smallpox was spread when a sick person came into contact with a healthy person. Leaders in Boston realized that many sick people arrived aboard ship. In 1647 city authorities enacted laws quarantining infected ships in Boston Harbor. Only when the last crusty scabs had fallen off—or the dead were buried or dis-

posed of at sea—could the ships dock. The quarantine measures met with some success and were later adopted by other communities. But since merchants made no profit until they could unload and sell their goods, many infected ships slipped through.

When smallpox made landfall, it spread like dominoes falling: sailors infected dockhands, who infected their families, who infected their neighbors. Doctors and clergy caring for the sick unknowingly carried the disease from house to house. Traders moving between communities brought it with them on their journeys. And in some cases, skirmishes between enemies allowed smallpox to jump from one area to another.

One such case was King William's War. In 1690 the English and their Indian allies were fighting against the French and their Indian allies over land in Quebec. The English planned to attack Quebec on two sides, by land and by sea. They held a meeting with their Mohegan and Iroquois allies to outline the overland part of the attack. Some Mohegans as well as some English soldiers bore the scars of a recent smallpox infection, and some still carried the disease. They infected the Iroquois; three hundred died. The surviving Iroquois refused to take part in the campaign. The overland attack had to be abandoned.

Meanwhile, the overseas prong of the attack was setting out from Boston—a Boston in the last throes of a smallpox epidemic. By the time the English fleet arrived outside Quebec, the disease had taken hold of the soldiers on board.

The French, safe from an overland attack, fortified Quebec City as the fleet sailed toward them. When the fleet arrived, the French easily defeated the sickened English. Smallpox had helped Quebec remain in the hands of the French.

The first waves of Europeans who explored and settled in the New World faced challenges they never would have experienced had they stayed in their homelands. But these challenges were lessened in some ways because of smallpox. Smallpox removed much of the indigenous population, giving the settlers a virtually unobstructed entry into the New World. Might the Native Americans have resisted the European invaders if smallpox had not killed them in such vast numbers? That's a question smallpox made impossible for us to answer.

At the close of the seventeenth century, smallpox was as deadly and mystifying as ever. It would remain so for the next hundred years, killing thousands more before, at last, a ray of hope shone on the horizon.

CHAPTER FOUR

INOCULATION
❧ *and the* ❧
AMERICAN REVOLUTION

Inoculation has never been used in America, nor indeed in our nation,
but how many lives might be saved by it, were it practiced.
—*Diary of Cotton Mather, May 26, 1721*

 N MID-APRIL OF 1721 two ships from the West
Indies slipped past the quarantine site of Spectacle
Island in Boston Harbor. They made their way to the
Boston docks and began to unload cargo from their holds.

Smallpox had not struck Boston for nineteen years.
Children had been born and grown up without ever having
been exposed to the virus. Many younger adults had forgotten
what it was like to live through the terror of infection. Their
memories would soon be rekindled.

"The grevious calamity of the smallpox has now entered
the town," wrote the Reverend Cotton Mather (1663–1728).
Mather, a Puritan minister in Boston and son of Increase

Mather, had survived smallpox when he was fifteen and had witnessed the most recent outbreak in 1702. He had also heard of a procedure he believed might help prevent people from getting the disease. The procedure was called inoculation.

Inoculation, or variolation as it was also called, was the purposeful infection of a healthy person with smallpox pus from a mildly sick person. Although inoculation was new to Mather and most Europeans, many cultures had been practicing something similar for generations. The Chinese, for example, blew ground smallpox scabs up a person's nose. In India an operation that involved lancing an arm and mixing the blood with pus from a pox pustule had been practiced as early as the year 400. Parts of Africa were also familiar with inoculation, as Cotton Mather was to discover.

In 1706 Mather obtained an African slave named Onesimus. He asked Onesimus a number of questions, including whether or not he had ever had smallpox. Ten years later, Mather wrote about this conversation in a letter to Dr. John Woodward of London:

"I had from a servant of my own, an account of its [inoculation's] being practiced in Africa. Enquiring of my Negro-Man Onesimus, who is a pretty intelligent fellow, whether he ever had ye smallpox, he answered Yes and No; and then told me that he had undergone an operation, which had given him something of ye smallpox, and would forever preserve him from it, adding . . . whoever had ye courage to use it was forever free from ye fear of the contagion. He described ye operation to me, and showed me in his arm ye scar."

Mather was struck by the possibility that this operation, although risky, might help stop smallpox. When the smallpox epidemic broke out in Boston in 1721, he delivered a sermon to the physicians of the city entreating them to consider inoculation.

Most of the doctors refused to even entertain the idea. They, like most Bostonians, believed that God delivered smallpox as punishment for sin. To lessen the severity of smallpox through inoculation would be the same as questioning God's will. The religious outcry against inoculation—and Cotton Mather—was deafening.

People feared inoculation for another reason. Purposely infecting oneself seemed dangerous. Even supposing inoculation only gave patients a mild form of the disease, they could infect those around them—and thus create the very epidemic Mather hoped to prevent.

Only one doctor out of the ten who heard Mather's sermon listened. Zabdiel Boylston joined the minister in his fight for inoculation. On June 26, 1721, he inoculated his six-year-old son and two slaves, the first of many inoculations he was to perform.

When the physicians of Boston heard what Boylston had done, they were outraged. "I never saw the devil so let loose upon any occasion," wrote Mather of the fury unleashed upon himself and Boylston. Boylston was forced to hide out when gangs threatened to hang him. A crude bomb was thrown through Mather's window; it failed to explode, but the letter attached—"Cotton Mather, you dog. Damn you! I'll inoculate you with this, with a pox to you!"—spoke volumes.

Meanwhile, smallpox continued to rage through the streets of Boston and its outlying towns. Cambridge, home of Harvard University, was infected by the middle of July.

Cotton Mather's son, Samuel, was at Harvard then. Samuel had never had the disease. When his roommate died of smallpox, Samuel fled Harvard in fear for his life. He begged his father to inoculate him.

Suddenly, inoculation took on a whole new meaning for Cotton Mather. If Samuel were inoculated and died, Mather's opponents would never let him hear the end of it. But if he didn't inoculate Samuel, he would look like a hypocrite.

In the end, Mather inoculated Samuel, but privately so that as few people as possible knew of it. Samuel survived the epidemic.

The same could not be said of other Bostonians. As summer gave way to fall, the disease intensified. Activity in Boston ground to a halt. Shops closed. Streets were deserted except for mourners and the death cart rolling by at night. Funeral bells tolled endlessly. In one week alone, the number of sick in Cotton Mather's North Church congregation jumped from 202 to 322.

By late fall of 1721 Bostonians were so terrified of the disease that they were ready to try anything to stop it—even inoculation. Suddenly they only cared about one thing: did it work? As more and more successful inoculations were given, the hue and cry against the procedure grew quieter.

By January of 1722 the epidemic was nearly over. Of a population of 11,000, 5,800 people had been infected with the disease. Some 844 people, roughly one in six, had died. A new figure ran alongside these others: 280 people had been inoculated against the disease. Although 6 of these people died as a result of the inoculation, the others emerged from the epidemic unscathed.

THE LADY MARY WORTLEY MONTAGU

On April 1, 1717, Lady Mary Wortley Montagu, an English noblewoman living in Istanbul, Turkey, with her husband, the British ambassador, wrote a historic letter to her friend Sarah Chiswell in London. The letter described a process called ingrafting. This letter was England's introduction to inoculation. Lady Montagu wrote:

"The smallpox, so fatal, and so general amongst us, is here entirely harmless, by the invention of ingrafting. . . . [An] old woman comes with a nut-shell full of the matter of the best sort of small-pox, and asks what vein you please to have opened. She immediately rips open that you offer her, with a large needle (which gives you no more pain than a common scratch) and puts into the vein, as much matter as can lie upon the head of her needle, and after that binds up the little wound with a hollow bit of shell. . . . Every year thousands undergo this operation. . . . There is no example of anyone that had died in it."

Lady Montagu had survived smallpox when she was young, but she was badly scarred and left without eyebrows. She had lost a brother to the disease. When she heard of the procedure, she was quick to champion it. She had her son inoculated in 1718.

Dr. Charles Maitland performed the operation, which was a complete success. The following year the Montagus and Dr. Maitland returned to England. In 1721, when smallpox hit London, Dr. Maitland inoculated the Montagus' four-year-old daughter. It was the first professional inoculation performed in England.

Religious controversy and fear of inducing an epidemic surrounded the procedure at first. However, the British royal family, particularly Princess Caroline, supported inoculation. Lady Montagu continued to speak on its behalf as well. The cry against it slowly died down. By 1723 inoculations were being performed with regularity in England.

"I know nobody that has repented the operation," wrote Lady Montagu to her sister in 1723. Thanks to her efforts, people in England, and later the rest of Europe, were armed against smallpox for the first time.

The subject of inoculation, after creating such riotous outrage, fell out of the public eye as the number of smallpox cases in Boston diminished, then disappeared. But enough people had seen or heard of its benefits to spread the word. Inoculation was introduced in Philadelphia during an epidemic in 1730, in New York in 1731, and in Charleston, South Carolina, in 1738. By the mid-1700s inoculation had been accepted as a means of protection.

Still, the number of people inoculated was not high enough to prevent smallpox from continuing to torment. The poor, who could not afford the expensive procedure, suffered. African slaves who had been born in America often fell victim as well, as did many Native Americans. In fact, people in this last group, far from being inoculated, sometimes became targets of biological warfare.

THE FRENCH AND INDIAN WAR

By the early 1750s both France and England had greatly expanded their territories in the New World. Clashes over religion, trade, and land often sprang up where territories overlapped. In 1754 a conflict arose over which country had supremacy in the Ohio River valley. France needed to control this region because it was the link between its Canadian trading posts and those in Louisiana. Britain, on the other hand, felt it had a greater claim because the English settlers in the region far outnumbered the French.

The initial conflict over the Ohio River valley soon ballooned into a full-fledged war for domination in the New World. It became known as the French and Indian War (1754–1763), with the British pitted against the French and their Indian allies. Two years later, an extension of this struggle for domination broke out in Europe, with France and its European allies of Russia and Austria fighting for supremacy against Britain and Prussia. This conflict became known as the Seven Years' War (1756–1763).

The French and Indian War was fought on American and Canadian soil. Smallpox dogged both sides. Soldiers spread it to one another and passed it to their enemies. They carried it home and infected their families, who in turn gave it to other civilians. People fleeing infected cities brought smallpox with them to new regions. New England, Canada, New York, Pennsylvania, Virginia, South Carolina, and other areas were besieged by epidemics during the years of the French and Indian War.

The Indian tribes suffered as well. Sometimes they contracted the disease by accident, as happened when they looted Fort William Henry in upstate New York after the fort fell to the French in 1758. The English living in the fort were in the midst of a smallpox epidemic. The Indians soon came down with it. Many died.

But sometimes the Indians got smallpox because someone planned to give it to them. Two instances of this occurred in 1763.

That year, Chief Pontiac, an Ottawa Indian, led his tribe and several others in harassing English colonists in Pennsylvania, Maryland, and Virginia, a movement later known as Pontiac's Rebellion. At the end of May, the Mingo, Delaware, and Shawnee laid siege to the British stronghold of Fort Pitt in Pennsylvania.

After a month under siege, the British came up with a plot to end their entrapment by infecting the Indians with small-pox. Two blankets and a handkerchief or two were procured

Colonel Henry Bouquet may have tried to infect Indians with smallpox during the French and Indian War.

from smallpox victims and given to the Indians. "I hope it will have the desired effect," wrote William Trent, the commander of the local militia.

One month later a second, similar attempt was made. Historians believe that Baron Jeffrey Amherst, the commander in chief of the English forces, was unaware that the plan had been tried once before when he wrote of his idea to one of his officers, Colonel Henry Bouquet:

"Could it not be contrived to send the smallpox among these disaffected tribes of Indians? We must on this occasion use every strategem in our power to reduce them."

Colonel Bouquet wrote back: "I will try to inoculate the ———— with some blankets that may fall in their hands, and take care not to get the disease myself."

Whether Bouquet carried out his plan is not known for sure. However, a smallpox epidemic did break out among the besieging tribes at the time of this correspondence. The weakened Indian forces were defeated by the British, led by Colonel Bouquet, later that summer.

But as devastating as smallpox was during the French and Indian War, those outbreaks paled in comparison to how smallpox affected soldiers and civilians during the next great war: the American Revolution.

THE SIEGE OF BOSTON

Between 1775 and 1782, the years during which the American Revolution was fought, more than 155,000 people

SMALLPOX *in the* NEW WORLD

living in the United States and Canada died. An estimated 25,000 were killed during battles with the British. The rest, approximately 130,000, were killed by smallpox.

The great epidemic that swept through the fledgling United States during these years is usually overshadowed by the events of the Revolution. Yet many of those events were linked with smallpox.

One such event was the siege of Boston. In April 1775 British troops were defeated at Lexington and Concord in Massachusetts. They fled to Boston, closely followed by the colonial militia. The militia laid siege to the town, hoping to paralyze the British troops by cutting off their contact with Britain.

A smallpox epidemic raged throughout the siege. The New Englanders inside Boston were much more vulnerable than the British. Many British soldiers had been inoculated or were immune. Not so the Bostonians. "From ten to thirty funerals a day," wrote one person who survived the siege and the epidemic.

Such was the situation that confronted George Washington when he arrived to take charge of the Continental Army on July 2, 1775. He knew firsthand of the horrors of smallpox, for he himself had survived the disease when he was nineteen. He realized the effect smallpox could have on America's struggle against the British. It had the potential to wipe out large segments of the Continental Army camped outside Boston. And of course, continuing sickness and death would distract civilians and soldiers from the cause.

Washington seriously considered inoculation as a means of protecting his soldiers against smallpox. But there were problems with inoculation. After the operation, a person was bedridden and quarantined for days. If Washington inoculated the bulk of his army at the same time, the army would be incapacitated. But if he inoculated in stages, the soldiers who were not inoculated were at risk of contracting the disease from those who were unless a strict quarantine was observed.

Washington finally decided against inoculation—for the time being.

Meanwhile smallpox continued its attack on Boston. In early November the British commanders seem to have tried to use the disease to their advantage.

"General Howe has ordered 300 inhabitants of Boston to Point Shirley in destitute condition," Washington wrote to Congress on November 27, 1775. "[I] am under dreadful apprehensions of their communicating the Smallpox as it is rife in Boston." Anxious to prevent a debilitating outbreak, Washington ordered those fleeing Boston to stay clear of the Continental Army and to remain under supervision until declared pox-free.

His measures seem to have worked, for smallpox did not break out among the American forces near Boston. In the end it was General Howe who broke, surrendering Boston to the Americans on March 17, 1776.

THE ETHIOPIAN REGIMENT

On November 7, 1775, as British troops lay under siege in Boston, Lord Dunmore, the Loyalist governor of Virginia, made a stunning proclamation. He issued an order freeing any slave or indentured servant willing to join forces against the Americans. Dunmore's act appalled and terrified Virginia slaveholders, including George Washington. A regiment made up of people they had enslaved might be a deadly threat.

The Ethiopian regiment, as Dunmore's troops were called, soon numbered nearly one thousand former slaves and servants. As a fighting force, however, it was not very effective. After a defeat near Norfolk, Virginia, in December 1775, Dunmore moved his troops to a flotilla of boats. This flotilla became his base camp. It would prove to be a ripe breeding ground for smallpox.

Once on board, the disease spread like wildfire. Dunmore and his soldiers stayed afloat for two months, but eventually he was forced to sail ashore. From February to May 1776, the regiment camped at Tucker's Point in Virginia. Smallpox camped with them.

Lord Dunmore commanded a doomed regiment of freed slaves and indentured servants.

Dunmore finally decided to inoculate those who were not sick. He couldn't do it at Tucker's Point, however, because the site was too vulnerable to attack. So in May he moved his troops yet again, this time to Gwynn's Island. Left behind at Tucker's Point were the graves of three hundred pox-riddled corpses.

Slaves continued to join Dunmore's regiment. "Had it not been for this horrid disorder, I should have had two thousand blacks; with whom I should have had no doubt of penetrating into the heart of this Colony," Dunmore wrote in June. As it was, by the time smallpox had finished with the men of the Ethiopian regiment, they numbered fewer than three hundred.

Lord Dunmore fled with those three hundred during an attack on the island on July 9. Five hundred bodies, some buried in mass graves, some burned, others left to rot, and even a few still clinging to life, covered the island when the Patriot troops landed to secure it.

Survivors spread smallpox when they escaped up the Potomac River. Deserters took it even farther inland, until the infection had reached the far corners of Virginia.

THWARTED IN QUEBEC

Even as the disease lingered in Boston and moved throughout Virginia, it found its way into Canada. In late fall of 1775, Quebec was in the hands of the British. Quebec was a key location; whoever controlled it controlled Canada.

In late November and early December, the Continental Army approached Quebec from the east and from the south. The soldiers set up camp outside the city—more than one

Hundreds of Continental soldiers were laid low by smallpox during their attempted siege of Quebec.

SMALLPOX *in the* NEW WORLD

thousand exhausted, weakened men crammed together in filthy quarters in the dead of winter.

Smallpox couldn't have asked for better conditions. "The small pox is all around us," wrote Caleb Haskell, a fife player, on December 6, 1775. And later, "I am very ill . . . no bed to lie on; no medicine to take; troubled much with a sore throat."

Haskell survived, but others were not so lucky. Smallpox raced through the camp, sending hundreds of men to their beds and many to their graves. For some soldiers, outlasting smallpox was a race against time. Many troops from New England were finishing their tour of duty as of the first of the year. If they could stay alive until January 1, 1776, they could return home.

The leader of the force, General Richard Montgomery, realized his campaign was in jeopardy. He decided to take action before the New England soldiers were discharged, and before more troops were taken ill. On December 31, 1775, in a raging blizzard, he launched his attack.

It was a dismal failure. Montgomery died in the assault, as did thirty other Americans. Four hundred more became prisoners of war.

Smallpox continued to wage its own war, this time against the prisoners and their guards. Eighty enlisted men were sick by mid-January. The officers, housed apart from the enlisted and given better food, clothing, and quarters, fared better. Sixteen were even inoculated.

Outside Quebec's walls, the remaining American forces tried to lay siege to the city. Benedict Arnold, in charge of the troops after Montgomery's death, repeatedly called for reinforcements. By March 30 his forces had grown from 800 men to 2,505—but 786 of those had smallpox. By the first week of May, only 1,900 soldiers remained, and 900 of them were sick with the pox.

That same week, British reinforcements reached Quebec. They immediately attacked the American troops, now under the command of Major General John Thomas. Weakened and unprepared, Thomas's forces fled. Thomas surrendered; Quebec, and Canada, remained in the hands of the British.

THE DECISION TO INOCULATE

Throughout these campaigns and for months afterward, George Washington struggled with the problem of whether to inoculate his troops. Finally, in January 1777, he made his decision. He wrote of it to Dr. William Shippen, Jr., the medical director of the army:

"Finding the smallpox to be spreading much, and fearing no precaution can prevent it from running through the whole of our Army, I have determined that the troops shall be inoculated . . . I would faine hope . . . that in a short space of time we shall have an Army not subject to this the greatest of all calamities that can befall it."

On February 12, 1777, the Continental Congress passed a resolution authorizing the inoculation. Army doctors began the procedure almost immediately. Thousands of soldiers and civilians were inoculated that year.

For the most part, all went well, or so Washington thought. Then, during the harsh winter at Valley Forge in 1778, he learned that nearly four thousand soldiers had not been inoculated. Washington ordered them to undergo the procedure, with the result that in the late winter of 1778, hundreds of men were in bed recovering rather than at their posts.

A meeting of the
Continental Congress
soon after France
entered the war

At the same time new recruits, who could have swelled the army's ranks, were also bedridden at the inoculation centers. These soldiers were tended by men immune to the disease—men Washington desperately needed close at hand and ready to fight. Finally Washington decided that rather than have all new troops inoculated in remote locations before joining their units, he would have them inoculated once they had arrived. That way, once the inoculated soldiers were well, they could be put to use immediately.

It was a risky decision: if even one inoculated soldier was released from his sickbed while he was still contagious, he could spread the disease to the uninoculated. But it was a chance Washington felt had to be taken. Fortunately, the change in policy had no ill effects.

The number of outbreaks among the troops dropped considerably after the mass inoculation. When France entered the war, its military power helped tip the balance in favor of the Americans. Had Washington not inoculated the troops, however, just the opposite might have happened—the French soldiers could very well have brought smallpox with them and infected their American allies. Without inoculation, the American Revolution might have ended quite differently.

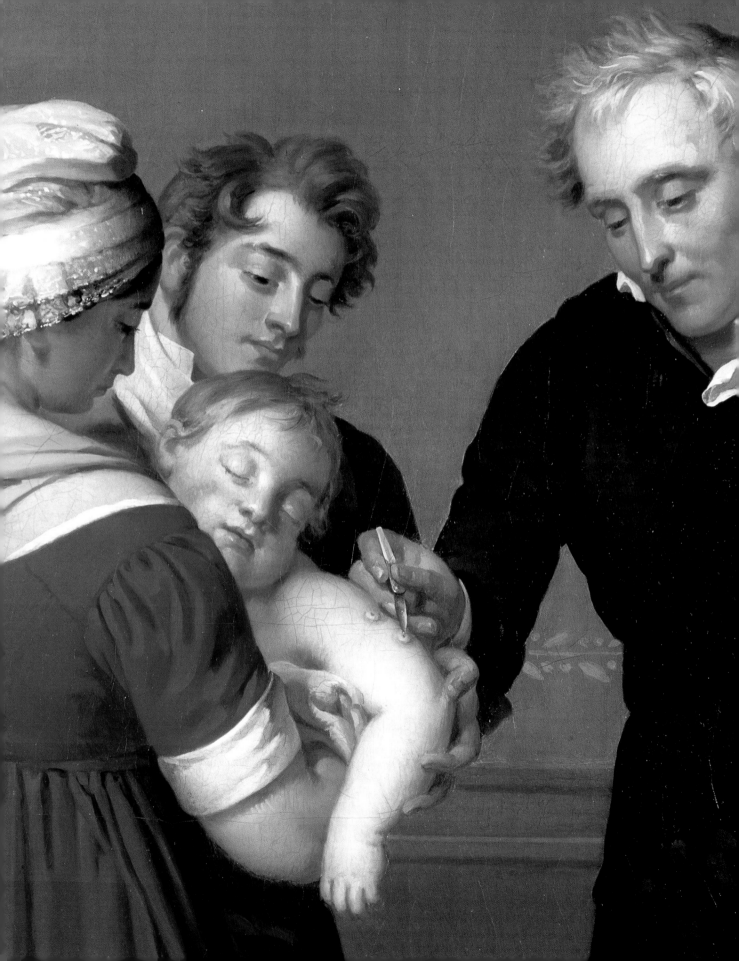

CHAPTER FIVE

The BEGINNING *of the* END

In the present age of scientific investigation it is remarkable that a disease of so peculiar a
nature as the cow-pox, which has appeared in this and some of the neighbouring counties
for such a series of years, should so long have escaped particular attention.
—*Letter from Edward Jenner to C. H. Parry, June 21, 1798*

BY THE END OF THE EIGHTEENTH CENTURY, inoculation had proven its worth. But despite all the good it brought, it had drawbacks. Those inoculated were still sickened by the disease—a few even died from it. Sometimes infection of a different nature would spring up at the inoculation site.

What was needed was a way to acquire immunity without actually giving people smallpox. In 1796 an Englishman named Edward Jenner found that way.

EDWARD JENNER AND VACCINATION
Edward Jenner was born in Berkeley, England, on May 17,

Opposite:
A doctor examines the pustules that formed after vaccination with cowpox.

1749. When he was eight years old, smallpox struck Gloucestershire, the county where he lived. Since the deaths of his parents three years earlier, Edward was being raised by his brother Stephen. As the disease was taking its toll in the county, Stephen decided to have Edward inoculated. It took more than a month for Edward to recover, an experience the boy would never forget.

When Edward was thirteen, he became a doctor's apprentice. He moved to London at age twenty-one to continue studying medicine. Two years later, he returned to his hometown to serve as its doctor.

As a child, Jenner had heard tales that milkmaids couldn't get smallpox if they had had cowpox. Cowpox was caught after milking a cow with cowpox pustules on its udder. Cowpox was similar to smallpox, but much less severe. Days after contact, pustules appeared on the hands and the patient experienced fever, nausea, and a week of discomfort.

Jenner became intrigued by the possibility that smallpox and cowpox were related. If so, would it be possible for a person purposely infected with cowpox to become immune to smallpox? He decided to put his theory to the test.

On May 14, 1796, Jenner took some pus from cowpox blisters on the hands of a milkmaid named Sarah Nelmes. He then made a small cut in the arm of an eight-year-old boy named James Phipps and applied the cowpox pus to it. A few days later, James came down with cowpox.

After James recovered, Jenner took the experiment to the next step. On July 1, 1796, Jenner inoculated Phipps with smallpox. Then he waited to see if Phipps would develop smallpox. Days passed, but Phipps remained healthy.

Jenner was ecstatic. He was sure James was immune to

smallpox because of the cowpox infection. He wrote a report of his discovery to the Royal Society of London. But the prestigious scientific organization was unimpressed and refused to publish Jenner's paper. Regardless of the snub, Jenner was convinced he was on to something. For two more years, he experimented with cowpox and smallpox. In 1798 he published his own paper under the title *An Inquiry into the Causes and Effects of the Variolae Vaccinae.* In it he used the term *vaccine* to describe the pus he had taken from Sarah Nelmes. *Vaccine* means "from a cow" in Latin. After Jenner's publication, it came to mean something much more.

Although plenty of people were resistant to the idea of putting pus from a cow into their bodies, many were scared enough of smallpox to risk it. Two years after Jenner published his paper, the king and queen of England bestowed their approval on vaccination, as Jenner's procedure was being called.

Word of Jenner's success spread throughout Europe. His publication was translated into several languages. Eventually it made its way overseas to the newly created United States, where it reached the hands of Dr. Benjamin Waterhouse of Massachusetts.

VACCINATION COMES TO THE NEW WORLD

Benjamin Waterhouse had an impressive medical background. He had been a doctor's apprentice from age sixteen to age twenty-one, when he sailed to Britain to continue his studies at Edinburgh. In 1780 he received his M.D. degree from Leiden University in Holland. He returned to the United States in 1781. A year later he became one of three professors of medicine at Harvard's new medical school.

When Waterhouse read Jenner's publication, he immedi-

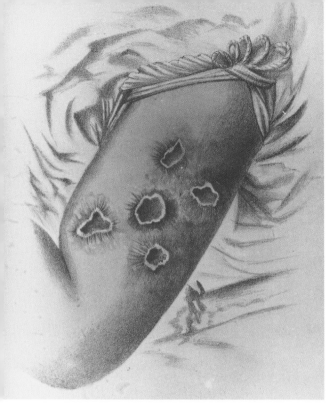

An arm with smallpox pustules. The similarities between cowpox and smallpox pustules led Jenner to his theory that the two diseases were related.

ately recognized its importance. He was eager to begin experimenting with vaccination in the United States.

But acquiring the vaccine was not easy. In order for it to be effective, the vaccine had to be harvested from cowpox blisters at a certain time in their development—too soon or too late would yield a weak and ineffective vaccine. Finding blisters in the first place was a difficulty, too, because there was no way of knowing when or where cowpox was going to turn up.

Jenner had recognized these difficulties himself early on in his experimentation. Rather than ferreting out milkmaids with cowpox blisters or the cows themselves, he harvested and stored pus taken from sores that developed on people he had vaccinated. This pus would then become the vaccine that would create more pus, and so on. He also experimented with arm-to-arm vaccinations, taking pus from active sores of a vaccinated person and using it immediately on another person.

Waterhouse was fortunate to receive a supply of vaccine from a doctor friend in England. In July 1800 he performed the first vaccinations in the United States—on his five-year-old son and six other people in his household. When his son proved immune to smallpox following an inoculation, Waterhouse was convinced that Jenner's vaccination worked.

Waterhouse's delight with the vaccine's success may not have been purely humanitarian. Although he was a respected physician, he was not wealthy. He may have thought he had a chance to make a good deal of money by first spreading the word about vaccination, then cornering the market on vaccine.

Documents show that he charged a huge sum for each vaccination he gave, and that he refused to share his supply of vaccine with colleagues. But his efforts to control the sale and supply of the smallpox vaccine failed. By mid-October 1800 several other doctors in New England had obtained vaccine from England.

Yet Waterhouse still made a name for himself. In a letter to Vice President Thomas Jefferson, he requested that he be appointed to bring vaccine to states south of New England, which had yet to receive any. Jefferson agreed, replying in his letter of December 25, 1800, that "every friend of humanity must look with pleasure on this discovery, by which one evil more is withdrawn from the condition of man."

Waterhouse sent three shipments of vaccine to Jefferson, two of which proved ineffective, perhaps because they had been destroyed in transit. The third was viable. It spearheaded the vaccination campaign outside New England as doctors in Washington, D.C., Baltimore, Philadelphia, and New York put it to use.

In the following years, Waterhouse continued to promote vaccination—and to make enemies. His colleagues in Boston still resented him for trying to capitalize on the early years of vaccination. Waterhouse did little to endear himself to his fellow physicians. He insisted that he had not tried to create a monopoly. Rather, he claimed he had held back the vaccine because he wanted to be sure that whoever was entrusted with it knew how to use it properly.

Such concern would not have been unfounded. There had been cases in which someone was accidentally vaccinated with smallpox instead of cowpox. That person contracted smallpox and when his or her pus was used as vaccine, it caused a smallpox infection. Just such a circumstance happened in Marblehead, Massachusetts, in October 1800. Sixty-eight people died in the smallpox outbreak that followed.

Whatever his true motivations, Waterhouse is nevertheless responsible for bringing vaccination to the United States. Without his continued efforts, the practice of vaccination might not have spread as quickly as it did.

Vaccination marked the beginning of the end of smallpox. As the nineteenth century progressed, improvements were made to the vaccine. In 1805 Italians had discovered that it was possible to grow cowpox in cows by mixing the virus into scratches in the animals' skin, then collecting the pus that developed. By the late nineteenth century, this was the most common method of creating vaccine. Now doctors in many parts of the world had access to a regular supply. Campaigns to vaccinate at-risk populations, such as children, abounded in many countries.

NATIVE AMERICANS: STILL ON THE FRINGE

Vaccination helped stem the outbreaks of smallpox in cities and towns, but epidemics continued to strike places in the world that the vaccine couldn't reach. Vaccine cost money, and many people were too poor to afford it. And those living in remote rural areas of the United States, such as the outer edges of the new country's frontier, simply didn't have access to the vaccine and so were vulnerable when the virus came their way.

Efforts were made to vaccinate the always vulnerable Native Americans. When a group of Native Americans, representing several tribes, visited Thomas Jefferson in Washington in 1801, the president gave them a supply of vaccine to take home. In 1807 Edward Jenner sent the Abenaki tribe a book

outlining vaccination. The Abenaki received the book with thanks, writing to Jenner that they would "not fail to teach our children to speak the name of Jenner and to thank the Great Spirit for . . . bestowing upon him so much wisdom." Congress set aside $12,000 in 1832—a considerable sum then—for the sole purpose of vaccinating Native Americans.

However, many tribes remained suspicious of the white man's motives and refused to be vaccinated. For others, especially in the West, the vaccine remained inaccessible even if they wanted to use it. These tribes were often the hardest hit when smallpox struck them. Each new epidemic left hundreds dead and in some cases whole tribes annihilated.

One such epidemic occurred in 1837. It started with two sick sailors aboard a cargo vessel sailing up the Missouri River. The captain stopped the boat near the Mandan tribe's encampment to trade. When the chiefs came on board, they caught smallpox. When they returned, they infected their people.

Death continued to haunt Indian tribes even after vaccination was introduced.

The disease spread like wildfire through the Mandans. "Nobody thought of burying the dead," wrote artist George Catlin, who witnessed the tragedy. "Whole families together were left in horrid and loathsome piles in their own wigwams, with a few buffalo robes thrown over them, there to decay, and be devoured by their own dogs."

Only thirty or forty Mandans out of two thousand survived.

From the Mandans the disease spread to the Blackfeet, the Cheyenne, and the Crows. An estimated 25,000 died in less than half a year. In the wake of this tragedy came the white pioneers, pushing westward across the United States. As had happened more than two hundred years earlier when the Pilgrims came to Massachusetts, the whites moved in virtually unchallenged and claimed the land for their own.

A DREAD DISEASE SLOWLY DIES

As the nineteenth century drew to a close, more and more nations around the world vaccinated their people. In 1895 Sweden proclaimed that smallpox no longer existed within its borders. In 1899 mass vaccinations in Puerto Rico ended the disease that had wiped out its native population centuries earlier. The Philippines, the Soviet Union, and Great Britain all proclaimed smallpox eradicated from their countries in the 1930s. Ten years later, the United States declared itself free of the disease.

Yet as long as the disease roamed the earth, the threat of epidemic persisted. Vaccinations lasted only seven to ten years, it had been discovered; if people didn't get revaccinated, they were at risk.

Just such a scare happened in New York City in 1947. A businessman fell ill and died of what doctors first thought was acute bronchitis. When word got out that he had died of smallpox, panic erupted.

City officials were quick to step forward. They launched a massive month-long vaccination campaign. Nearly three and a half million New Yorkers were revaccinated during that time. Fortunately, no new cases of smallpox occurred.

This smallpox scare and others like it eventually convinced the United Nations to launch a worldwide campaign against the disease. The World Health Organization began its two-pronged attack against smallpox in 1967. The eradication program would take more than a decade, but in the end it worked.

ACCIDENTAL SMALLPOX IN THE TWENTIETH CENTURY

On November 28, 1977, a man living in Somalia made a journey that was noted by medical communities around the world. The journey wasn't far—he traveled only from an isolation area to his hometown. What was remarkable was that this man had just recovered from the last known case of naturally occurring smallpox in the world. His successful return to his family marked the end of smallpox.

He was not the last person to ever have smallpox, however, only the last one to contract the disease from nature rather than in a controlled setting. Individuals working in or near the laboratories that store the variola virus have since contracted smallpox after accidentally being exposed to it.

One such person was Janet Parker. Parker was a medical photographer at the University of Birmingham, England. She worked one floor above the medical school's animal poxvirus lab. In May 1978, two years before smallpox was eradicated and most stores of the virus destroyed, the lab had received a sample of a strain of variola virus taken from a Pakistani boy. On August 11, 1978, Parker went home sick, plagued with fever, chills, nausea, and aches. Ten days later she was covered with a red blistering rash. Janet Parker had smallpox. She died on September 11.

Authorities were frantic. After Parker's diagnosis, they quickly identified, isolated, and vaccinated anyone who had come into contact with her during her illness. Some experienced side effects from the vaccination. Her father died of a heart attack after being hospitalized for a fever. Her mother developed a mild smallpox rash and was quarantined. She later recovered, as did eight other people who were hospitalized as a precaution.

But the tragedy had claimed another life. Professor Henry S. Bedson was in charge of the poxvirus lab. It was he who identified Parker's particular strain of variola as having come from his lab. Realizing that he was ultimately responsible for her illness sent him into a tailspin of depression. On September 1 he slashed his throat with a knife. The note near his body read, "I am sorry to have misplaced the trust which so many of my friends and colleagues have placed in me and my work. . . . I realize this act is the least sensible I have done, but it may, I hope in the end, allow [my family] to get some peace."

The TERROR *of* BIOTERRORISM

MALLPOX HAD ROAMED THE EARTH FOR CENTURIES. It had wiped out civilizations. It had cleared the way for Europeans to explore, conquer, and colonize the Americas, giving them free rein to forge new civilizations out of the ruins of the old. Would Canada, Mexico, and the United States be what they are today without the interference of smallpox? There is no answer to this question, or to the question of what was lost when native populations were destroyed by the wrath of smallpox.

What would happen if smallpox were released from those frozen vials of stock in Atlanta and Moscow? Many people living today have never been vaccinated because they were

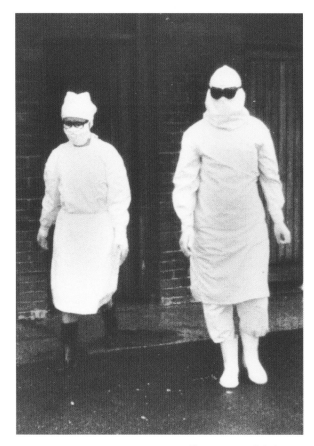

Laboratory workers dealing with smallpox wear protective clothing from head to toe.

born after smallpox was declared dead. The bulk of the world's population has no immunity because it has never been exposed to the virus. In other words, we'd have no more resistance to the disease than the Aztecs, the Incas, or the countless other Native American tribes that died of it.

After the terrorist attacks on September 11, 2001, health officials and members of the U.S. government confronted the possibility that smallpox could be used as a biological terrorist weapon. There had been rumors that stores of smallpox virus existed outside of the controlled labs in the United States and Russia. If that were true, then there was a possibility that smallpox could be unleashed on the world. How would the world respond?

Even before September 11, the Centers for Disease Control (CDC) in Atlanta had considered an answer to this question. The CDC's first response after the terrorist attacks was to call for the manufacture of smallpox vaccine. Production of the vaccine had all but halted after smallpox was eradicated; at the time of the attacks there was only a limited supply. Even though it is unlikely that smallpox will strike again, the CDC preferred to err on the side of caution. Pharmaceutical companies stepped up production. As of this writing, there are sufficient supplies of vaccine to protect everyone in the United States—but not the rest of the world.

SMALLPOX *in the* NEW WORLD

The CDC has also tackled the problem of what to do if a case of smallpox is discovered. Doctors, being on the front lines of medical problems, are at the heart of the solution. First, they have to recognize what they are seeing. Few doctors today have ever encountered a case of smallpox, so they need as much information about the disease as possible. The CDC has seen to this by updating its publications on the disease and stepping up their circulation.

Second, doctors have to work quickly to isolate and control a case, should one crop up. They've been instructed to inform local and state health officials and the CDC so that those agencies can step in to stop an outbreak, inform the public, and control public panic. Finally, the CDC and the doctors would need to vaccinate all who might have come into contact with the victim.

We live in a world without smallpox—and it seems unlikely that anyone will ever experience the terror this silent killer caused our ancestors. Still, it is a comfort to know that a response is in place. As watchful eyes keep guard over our health, we can only hope that that response will never be needed.

SMALLPOX THROUGH TIME

C. 3000 B.C.
Ancient Egyptian documents record smallpox-like disease

C. 1500 B.C.
Ancient Indian documents record smallpox-like disease

C. 1350 B.C.
Hittite empire nearly wiped out by epidemic

1157 B.C.
Pharaoh Ramses V dies of smallpox-like disease

430 B.C.
Smallpox-like disease strikes Athens, Greece

164
The Plague of Antonine

C. 250
Hunpox enters China

C. 310
Ko Hung describes Chinese epidemic

570
The Elephant War is won by Arabs after smallpox decimates Abyssinian troops

581
Gregory, bishop of Tours, describes epidemic in southern France and northern Italy

583
Smallpox enters Korea from China

585
Smallpox enters Japan with Korean Buddhist monks

C. 910
Rhazes writes treatise on smallpox and measles

Mid-1200s
Denmark and Iceland infected with smallpox

1430
Greenland colony wiped out

1438
Epidemic in Paris kills 50,000

1507
Epidemic on Hispaniola kills hundreds of indigenous population

1518
Second epidemic on Hispaniola kills most of the survivors of first epidemic; Cuban epidemic kills thousands of natives

1519
Epidemic on Puerto Rico kills half of native population

1520
Smallpox enters Aztec empire

1521
Cortés conquers Aztec empire

1524–1527
Epidemic rages through Inca empire

1527–1532
Civil war waged in Inca empire

1533
Pizarro conquers Inca empire; epidemic in Quito

1535
Epidemic in Quito

1576
Epidemic kills 2 million Indians in Mexico

1585
Epidemic in Peru

1613
Epidemic in Nagasaki, Japan, kills more than two thousand

1617–1619
Epidemic in Massachusetts wipes out nine-tenths of native population

1620
Pilgrims land at Plymouth

1633
Epidemic rages through New England, killing thousands of Native Americans and twenty colonists

1633–1634
  Narraganset and other tribes along Connecticut River struck down by smallpox
1636
  Boston epidemic
1640
  Iroquois League struck by smallpox
1640–1647
  Epidemic among the Huron Confederacy
1647
  First quarantine laws enacted in Boston
1648
  Iroquois defeat Huron
1649
  Iroquois epidemic
1659
  Boston epidemic
1663
  Iroquois epidemic
1666
  Boston epidemic
1677–1678
  Boston epidemic
1679
  Iroquois epidemic
1689–1690
  Boston epidemic
1690
  Outbreak before battle for Quebec in King William's War
1697–1698
  Boston epidemic
1702
  Boston epidemic
1716
  Letter from Cotton Mather regarding Onesimus's account of inoculation
1721–1722
  Boston epidemic; Cotton Mather recommends inoculation in Boston; Zabdiel Boylston performs first inoculation in America
1730
  Inoculation introduced in Philadelphia during an epidemic

1731
  Inoculation introduced in New York
1738
  Inoculation introduced in Charleston, South Carolina
1763
  Baron Jeffrey Amherst writes letter suggesting giving Native Americans smallpox
1775–1776
  Epidemic during siege of Boston; most of Ethiopian regiment dies of smallpox in Virginia; American forces outside Quebec struck by smallpox and suffer defeat
1777–1778
  Washington inoculates all American troops
1796
  Edward Jenner vaccinates James Phipps with cowpox
1800
  Benjamin Waterhouse vaccinates his son and other household members in the United States
1832
  Congress appropriates $12,000 for vaccination of Native Americans
1837
  Epidemic wipes out Mandan tribe
1895
  Sweden declares smallpox eradicated within its borders
1899
  Puerto Rico free of smallpox
1967
  WHO campaign to eradicate smallpox begins
1977
  Last case of naturally occurring smallpox
1978
  Janet Parker dies after contracting smallpox in lab
1980
  WHO declares smallpox dead
2001
  Terrorist attacks raise questions about the world's safety from biological weapons such as smallpox

GLOSSARY

alchemist a person who practices alchemy, an imaginary art of changing common metals into gold

conquistador the Spanish word for "conqueror"; usually applied to the men who conquered Mexico, South and Central America, and other regions in the sixteenth century

cowpox a disease caused by a virus that produces sores on the udders of cows. Jenner's smallpox vaccine was made from cowpox virus.

endemic disease a disease that is always present in a society

epidemic disease a disease that moves in, kills a vast number of people, then dies out

immunity the ability of the body to resist attacks by viruses and bacteria

inoculation the practice of purposely infecting a person with a mild form of a disease to create immunity

Loyalist a person who remained loyal to the English monarchy during the American Revolution; generally, someone who remains loyal to the established government during times of revolution

mutate to change or be altered

orthopox virus a family of viruses that infect animals and humans, including chicken pox, insect pox, monkey pox, and smallpox

pustule a raised sore filled with pus that appears on the skin

vaccination the purposeful injection of a live or dead virus or bacteria into the body to protect the body from a particular disease

vaccine live or dead virus, bacteria, or other chemicals that are injected into the body to produce immunity

variola the virus that causes smallpox

virus a submicroscopic parasite that must invade the cells of a host body in order to reproduce. When a virus infects enough cells, it causes disease.

TO FIND OUT MORE

BOOKS

Altman, Linda Jacobs. *Plague and Pestilence: A History of Infectious Disease.* Springfield, NJ: Enslow Books, 1998.

A well-written overview of a variety of diseases, including a section on smallpox.

Archer, Jules. *Epidemic! The Story of the Disease Detectives*. New York: Harcourt Brace Jovanovich, 1977.

An interesting look at the role of the epidemiologist in uncovering the causes of infectious disease. Includes a chapter on smallpox.

Hoff, Brent, and Carter Smith III. *Mapping Epidemics: A Historical Atlas of Disease*. New York: Franklin Watts, 2000.

An interesting book with maps and text that describes the spread of many infectious diseases, including smallpox.

Ridgway, Tom. *Smallpox Epidemics: Deadly Diseases through History*. New York: Rosen Publishing Group, 2001.

A brief overview of smallpox for younger readers.

ON THE INTERNET*

"Smallpox" at

http://www.seercom.com/bluto/smallpox

A brief overview of the disease, its pathology, and its history.

"Smallpox" at

http://www.bt.cdc.gov/agent/smallpox/index.asp

The official smallpox site of the Centers for Disease Control.

Includes links to the CDC's current plan to combat smallpox in the event of a bioterrorist attack.

"Smallpox: Inoculation Vaccination Eradication" at

http://www.library.ucla.edu/libraries/biomed/smallpox

An online exhibit featuring articles and illustrations about the early fight against smallpox.

*All Internet sites were available and accurate when this book was sent to press.

BIBLIOGRAPHY

Fenn, Elizabeth A. *Pox Americana: The Great Smallpox Epidemic of 1775–82*. New York: Hill and Wang, 2001.

Giblin, James Cross. *When Plague Strikes*. New York: HarperCollins, 1995.

Hopkins, Donald. *Princes and Peasants: Smallpox in History*. Chicago: University of Chicago Press, 1983.

Jenner, Edward. *Vaccination against Smallpox*. Great Minds series. Amherst, NY: Prometheus Books, 1996.

Thucydides. *History of the Peloponnesian War*. Translated by Rex Warner. Middlesex, England: Penguin Books, 1954.

Tucker, Jonathan B. *Scourge: The Once and Future Threat of Smallpox*. New York: Atlantic Monthly Press, 2001.

Winslow, Ola Elizabeth. *A Destroying Angel: The Conquest of Smallpox in Colonial Boston*. Boston: Houghton Mifflin, 1974.

NOTES ON QUOTATIONS

The quotations in this book are from the following sources:

Chapter One: What Is Smallpox?

p. 1: "Words indeed fail," Thucydides, *History of the Peloponnesian War*, p. 153.

p. 6: "People in perfect health," Ibid., p. 153.

p. 7: "Recently there have been," Hopkins, *Princes and Peasants*, p. 104.

p. 8: "A person, after being seized," Ibid., p. 24.

p. 9: "In the name of," Ibid., p. 101.

Chapter Two: Smallpox Conquers Mexico and South America

p. 11: "It became so great," Hopkins, *Princes and Peasants*, p. 206.

p. 17: "The victims were so covered," Ibid.

p. 20: "My father the Sun," Giblin, *When Plague Strikes*, p. 72.

p. 21: "They died by scores," Hopkins, *Princes and Peasants*, p. 213.

Chapter Three: Smallpox and the Early American Colonies

p. 23: "A few straggling inhabitants," Hopkins, *Princes and Peasants*, p. 235.

p. 26: "The Indians began," Giblin, *When Plague Strikes*, pp. 75–76.

p. 27: "They lye on their hard matts," Tucker, *Scourge*, p. 11.

p. 27: "Of a 1000, above 900," Fenn, *Pox Americana*, p. 23.

p. 28: "This disease has not been," Hopkins, *Princes and Peasants*, p. 236.

p. 28: "The small pox desolates them," Giblin, *When Plague Strikes*, p. 76.

Chapter Four: Inoculation and the American Revolution

p. 33: "Inoculation has never been," Winslow, *A Destroying Angel*, pp. 45–46.

p. 33: "The grevious calamity," Ibid., p. 45.

p. 34: "I had from a servant," Ibid., p. 33.

p. 35: "I never saw the devil" and "Cotton Mather, you dog," Hopkins, *Princes and Peasants*, p. 250.

p. 37: "The smallpox, so fatal," Ibid., pp. 47–48.

p. 37: "I know nobody," Giblin, *When Plague Strikes*, p. 83.

p. 40: "I hope it will," Tucker, *Scourge*, p. 20.

p. 40: "Could it not be contrived" and "I will try to inoculate," Hopkins, *Princes and Peasants,* p. 246.

p. 41: "From ten to thirty," Fenn, *Pox Americana,* p. 47.

p. 42: "General Howe has ordered," Ibid., p. 50.

p. 43: "Had it not been," Ibid., pp. 58–59.

p. 45: "The small pox is all around," and "I am very ill," Ibid., p. 63.

p. 46: "Finding the smallpox," Hopkins, *Princes and Peasants,* p. 261.

Chapter Five: The Beginning of the End

p. 49: "In the present age," Jenner, *Vaccination against Smallpox,* front matter.

p. 53: "every friend of humanity," Hopkins, *Princes and Peasants,* p. 265.

p. 55: "not fail to teach," Ibid., p. 270.

p. 56: "Nobody thought of," Giblin, *When Plague Strikes,* p. 100.

p. 58: "I am sorry," Tucker, *Scourge,* p. 129.

INDEX

**Page numbers for illustrations
are in boldface.**

ABOUT THE AUTHOR

STEPHANIE TRUE PETERS grew up in Westborough, Massachusetts. After graduating with a degree in history from Bates College, she moved to Boston, where she worked as an editor of children's books. She made the jump from editor to writer soon after the birth of her son. Since then she has authored a number of nonfiction books for young people, including the other titles in the Epidemic! series. Stephanie lives in Mansfield, Massachusetts, with her husband, Dan, and their two children, Jackson and Chloe. She enjoys going on adventures with her family, beachcombing on Cape Cod, and teaching kick-boxing classes at the local YMCA.